the accomplishments of today's quilters. Through its publications and events, AQS strives to honor today's quiltmakers and their work and to inspire future creativity and innovation in quiltmaking.

Executive Book Editor: Andi Milam Reynolds
Graphic Design: Lynda Smith
Cover Design: Michael Buckingham
Quilt Photography: Charles R. Lynch

Additional copies of this book may be ordered from the American Quilter's Society, PO Box 3290, Paducah, KY 42002-3290, or online at www.AmericanQuilter.com.

Text © 2009, Author, Cathy Wiggins
Artwork © 2009, American Quilter's Society

Library of Congress Cataloging-in-Publication Data

Wiggins, Cathy.
  Clowns on parade / by Cathy Wiggins.
    p. cm.
  ISBN 978-1-57432-998-8
  1. Appliqué--Patterns. 2. Patchwork--Patterns. I. Title.
  TT779.W557 2009
  746.44'5041--dc22

                    2009025421

American Quilter's Society
P. O. Box 3290 • Paducah, KY 42002-3290
www.AmericanQuilter.com

Dedication

I dedicate this book to my husband, Randy, who is always supportive through all of my quilting endeavors; to my daughter, Olivia, who is my single most important critic, design partner, and sounding board; and to all of those who have insisted that there are quilters waiting for patterns of these clowns.

Table of Contents

I have been asked at least a thousand times, "Where in the world did you get that idea?" by folks viewing my quilt CLOWNS ON PARADE. I always answer that question the same way, "Oh, it just sort of came to me." And it did, sort of.

I had the idea that it would be fun to create a pattern of a clown that could be embellished with a variety of items and three-dimensional elements. The problem was that when I started building on the idea, different clowns kept coming into my mind!

Before I knew it, I had eight different clowns and a monkey. Now what was I going to do? The driving force behind my clown quilt was to create something that would bring a smile and joy to everyone that viewed it. I thought that if one clown could make people smile, just think what eight could do! So I decided to put all eight clowns and the monkey on one quilt.

At this point, I had no idea how all of the clowns were going to fit together on a single quilt, but I knew that I would figure it out when the time came. This is the way that I usually create my quilts. I don't always figure out everything in the beginning. I just plan one step at a time, which leaves a lot of room for creativity and design changes.

I created each clown to the finished size of about 18 inches by 24 inches. This gave me plenty of room for all kinds of three-dimensional effects and individual embellishments as well as some extra quilting designs. I knew that these extra elements would add interest and enjoyment for the viewer and make the quilt special.

When the clowns and monkey were complete, I played around with them until I had a layout so they would all fit on a quilt that was less than 100 inches wide and allow room for some fun quilting designs and a border to frame the quilt. (The finished quilt had to be less than 110 inches wide due to the size restrictions of most quilt shows. I knew I would be entering this quilt in competitions!)

Because of the size of the clowns and the extra room I needed for the quilting, I didn't have much room for a border, so I had to get creative. This is how my unique ruffle border design came about. The finished size of the original CLOWNS ON PARADE quilt is 96 inches by 82 inches. You can make your quilt any size you like!

Since the creation of CLOWNS ON PARADE, many people have enjoyed spending time exploring the quilt and have asked for patterns of the clowns. These requests are what drove me to write this book. Nothing would give me more pleasure than to have hundreds of the clowns on quilts bringing joy to people—young and old alike.

As the clowns were created, they became individual characters in a scene to be displayed forever on a quilt. Let me introduce the clowns to you.

Little Bit balances on the ball and balances the plates on the poles.

Pablo the monkey adds his maracas to Sunshine's music.

Sunshine plays her horn so that there is music for all to enjoy.

Lu Lu is the sexy clown in the daisy swim suit.

Yum Yum's balloons help him with his handstand.

Hoss the cowboy leads the parade and pulls the first wagon.

Skinny holds the tub of water so Lu Lu can dive right in.

Bubbles rides a unicycle, juggles, and pulls the second wagon.

Boo Boo swings and smiles as the parade comes to an end.

My goal is to give you enough information to either re-create my clowns or, better yet, to give you enough ideas to allow you to create your own version of the clowns for those in your life to enjoy.

My hope is that you will use this book as an inspiration from which your own ideas grow. There are endless ways to create your version of these clowns, so just have fun and make the clowns your own. Let's get started!

Cathy Wiggins

Clowns on Parade

Layout of This Book

Each clown or monkey has his or her own chapter complete with a short biography, so that you can get to know each one a little better. The biographies explain the quilting designs, the three-dimensional elements, and the embellishments that accompany each character. You will also find suggestions for using each clown as a stand-alone individual on his or her own quilt. Remember, the biographies only explain the special effects that I have used. Use your imagination to create your own!

Following the biographies, you will find three sets of instructions: a pattern for each clown; patterns for the quilting designs; and directions for the three-dimensional elements.

Next you will find information on the wagons, poles, and the sign. There is a section on the ruffled border that I used on the original quilt, as well as binding and blocking hints.

Basic Supplies
Fabric

When I created this quilt, I did something that I have never done before; I constructed the entire quilt from fabrics found in my fabric stash. (Well, almost—I did have to buy fabric for the backing.) However, for those of you who must buy fabric before starting any new quilting project, I do have some basic fabric guidelines I followed when creating the clowns:

※ Select a fun print and a coordinating solid for each clown's costume. Multiple prints and solids can be used on a single costume, but try not to make the costumes too busy.

※ Remember that the hair is part of the costume, so have fun creating funky hair for your clowns.

※ Notice that I may have used many different fabrics. However, they are all bright, primary colors—reds, blues, greens, etc. (or any color that you would find in a small box of crayons).

※ If you are going to re-create the entire quilt, it is best to repeat each fabric at least twice in different areas of the quilt. This will help unify the design. For example, if you use a fabric for a shirt in one costume, use it for the pants of another.

※ You do not need to have a solid background. I put each clown on different fabrics ranging from yellow to orange.

Fusible Web

Any fusible web will work. Select your fusible web product based on the intended use of the finished quilt and how the top will be quilted. If the quilt will be used daily and lighter fusible webbing is used, the clown pieces will either need to be sewn down around the edges or heavily quilted to prevent the pieces from coming loose. If the quilt will be a wall hanging, the extra sewing done to secure the pieces may not be necessary.

I use HeatnBond® Lite iron-on adhesive. It is inexpensive and holds everything down until I am ready to sew it in place. I satin stitch around all of the pieces, and I also heavily quilt my quilts. Note that I do not rely on the fusible web to be the permanent holding solution.

Other Supplies

Other supplies I use for my appliqué technique when constructing the clowns include:

※ A black, fine-point Sharpie® permanent marker for tracing the patterns;

※ Small paper scissors for cutting the fusible web; and

※ A pressing surface as large as the pattern that I am working on. I usually use bath towels on top of my cutting table.

In addition to the above, you will need all of the usual basic sewing supplies.

Understanding the Patterns

The patterns for the clowns in this book are about 8 inches by 10 inches. However, all of the patterns can be enlarged to any size.

The clowns on the CLOWNS ON PARADE quilt are about 18 inches by 24 inches. Feel free to make your clowns any size that you wish. Just remember to enlarge all of the patterns that you will be using to the same size.

On the clown patterns, you will find both solid lines and dotted lines. If you choose to create your clowns without the three-dimensional elements, then ignore the dotted lines. These lines are used to complete the parts of the clowns that will be under the three-dimensional elements. (It is important to complete the parts under the three-dimensional elements so that when these elements are moved or lifted, there is a complete quilt underneath.)

Since some of the patterns have parts that extend beyond the page, such as Bubbles' unicycle and Little Bit's ball, I have included them separately on the pattern.

I also have included all of the defining (solid) lines such as the mouth, the lines that separate legs or arms, figure, etc. Once you have your fabrics fused in place, mark these lines with a chalk pencil and satin stitch them when you satin stitch the rest of the clown.

Keep in mind that the patterns for the quilting designs can also be used for fabric elements and appliqués and have been included in a larger scale than the clowns, so let your imagination soar when creating your clowns!

Close-up of Sunshine

Dotted lines indicate fabric edges behind three-dimensional elements. Defining (solid) lines indicate stitched lines that add interest to the figure.

Appliqué My Way

Because I use a fusible-web appliqué technique, I have to use a reverse image of the pattern for tracing the shapes on the fusible web.

To create the reverse image of the patterns from this book, first trace the pattern onto a piece of white drawing paper using the black Sharpie marker and label this side as "Piecing." Then turn the drawing paper over and trace the pattern again on the reverse side of the paper using the black Sharpie marker.

You should be able to see some of the lines from the other side bleeding through. This should help with tracing the reverse image. Label this side as "Tracing" and use it for tracing the fusible-web pieces. If you choose to enlarge your pattern, label the enlarged copy of the pattern as "Piecing." Turn it over and trace the lines on the other side to create the "Tracing" side. Once you have the reverse image of your pattern, you are ready to go.

1. Trace each section of the "Tracing" side of the pattern onto the fusible web. If the sections are large, you may choose to cut out the center of the web before ironing it onto the fabric to help eliminate stiffness.

2. Iron each of the sections onto the wrong side of the fabric that you have selected for that part of the pattern.

3. Cut each piece just outside of the tracing lines. By cutting just outside of the tracing

lines, you should have enough fabric to overlap a bit.

4. Place the pattern with the "Piecing" side up on top of the pressing surface and place the background fabric over it. If you have selected a light-colored fabric, you should be able to see the pattern through it. Since these patterns are rather simplistic, you may be able to assemble the pieces just by using the pattern as a guide instead of relying on seeing the pattern through the background fabric.

5. One at a time, put the fabric pieces in place and iron down.

Now your clowns are ready to complete as you choose! Note that my stitching didn't always follow the pattern perfectly, so you, too, can give your clowns any expression you choose!

Satin Stitching

I wanted my clowns to resemble a page from a child's coloring book, so I chose to outline all of my pieces with black satin stitching. Not only does this stitching help achieve the cartoon look, it also outlines and secures all fabric pieces; adds shapes, lines, and definition to the clowns; and attaches the clowns to the background fabrics.

To satin stitch, I use a mid-weight, tear-away stabilizer under the fabric; a 40-weight rayon thread on the top; and 40- or 50-weight cotton thread in the bobbin. I plan the satin stitching so that I sew over as many of the stops and

starts as I possibly can to secure the threads and prevent unraveling. I also trim the thread tails from the reverse side so that none will show through later.

Notice how I have used satin stitching to define Lu Lu's mouth, hand, arm, and eyelashes.

Three-dimensional Effects

There are three construction techniques used to create the three-dimensional elements for the clowns:

✻ Batting sandwich
✻ Fabric only
✻ Satin-stitched fusible

Batting Sandwich

I use the batting sandwich technique when I want to give the three-dimensional element thickness and body.

1. Cut each of the following using the supplied pattern, adding a ¼-inch seam allowance on all sides except on the edge that will be satin stitched:

a. One image from the fabric of your choice

b. The reverse image from the fabric of your choice

c. One image shape from batting

2. To eliminate the bulk when the element is attached to the quilt, trim the batting slightly from the edge.

3. Place the two fabric shapes right sides together. Place the batting shape on top and stitch the layers together with a ¼-inch seam, leaving the indicated edge open to allow for turning.

4. Trim seam allowances as close as possible without nipping seam stitches.

5. Turn right-side out and press.

Your batting sandwich is now ready to apply to your clown. I apply my sandwiches as I satin stitch the area. I satin stitch to the point the element is to be placed, hold the element in place, and then simply satin stitch over the element. This closes the open area. Then trim any frayed edges or stray threads.

Notice Bubbles' funky hair. It was created using the batting sandwich technique. The ruffled collar was created using the fabric-only technique.

Fabric Only

I use the fabric-only technique when several layers of fabric will be folded to form texture. Follow the same steps for this technique as for the batting sandwich, but do not use the batting.

Satin-Stitched Fusible

I use the statin-stitched fusible technique when I want to add textue but maintain the cartoon look. For these two-sided, satin-stitched elements, follow these steps:

1. Using the fusible web, fuse two pieces of fabric wrong sides together.

2. Using the pattern, cut out the desired shapes.

3. Satin stitch around all edges except the one marked "open" on the pattern.

4. Apply the element by satin stitching the open edge in place. Trim any frayed edges or stray threads.

I used the satin-stitched fusible technique on Sunshine's hair. I cut out multiple fabric pieces and added them all as I satin stitched around the face.

"No job is too big if you have a little help."

HOSS was the first clown I created. Since he had a horse, he had to be doing something besides just walking. Why not have him pull a wagon with poles for the other clowns in the parade to play on while they entertain us! And since he was my first clown, I gave him the honor of leading the parade.

Quilting Designs

With all of the responsibility of leading the parade as well as pulling a wagon, Hoss needed all the help he could get. This is why you find carrots hanging in front of his horse's head. I have always heard that if you put a carrot on a stick and hold it just in front of a horse's head, he would follow it. In addition to the help from the carrots, Hoss has the assistance of a little fairy dust from Eleanor, flying just behind him.

However, there could be trouble for Hoss that very few people see. Pablo has eaten part of one of his bananas and has dropped the rest on the path right under Hoss's foot and in front of the wagon. I do hope that it doesn't upset the parade!

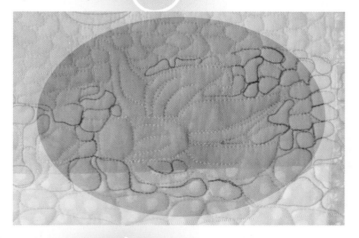

Three-dimensional Effects

I have given Hoss three-dimensional flaps around his horse's body. If you were to look underneath the flaps, you would find that Hoss is wearing pants.

Since pulling the wagon is hard work, I wanted to give him a nice pulling loop that would support the wagon weight.

Embellishments

The horse's bridle and reins are included in the pattern. However, I chose to use real rope in red and blue with a daisy flower at the center. Hoss also has a cute smiley button on his collar, but he would look just as cool with a western style tie. And I added a nice, thick rope through his loop and attached it to the wagon.

Layout Options

If Hoss is going solo on your quilt, he probably won't need the pulling loop. If you think that he still may need the carrots, simply add a stick coming from the top to the horse's head and attach the carrots to it. If quilting the carrots doesn't appeal to you, use the quilting design as an appliqué pattern.

Three-dimensional Elements

The flaps on Hoss are constructed using the batting sandwich method. Use the rectangle flaps on the pattern as your template and attach them as you satin stitch the bottom of the horse.

The pulling loop on Hoss is constructed using the satin-stitched fusible method. However, you could use a simple loop of string or thin rope instead.

"Don't hate me because I'm beautiful."

Lu Lu   Oh Lu Lu! What can you say about Lu Lu? I have found that people, ladies especially, relate to Lu Lu more than to any of the other clowns. Personally, I think that we all should put on our bathing suits and wear them proudly, just like Lu Lu does. Maybe if we paint our faces and put on a clown nose, it would make it more fun.

On the first design, Lu Lu had beautiful flowing blond hair, just like we all used to dream about having when we were little girls. But it was getting in her eyes and caught around her nose, so I decided to put it all under that lovely flowered swim cap.

Quilting Designs

Lu Lu was a little concerned about flying gracefully through the air if and when she made her dive, so I decided to help her with positive thinking. I gave her three butterflies to focus on and think, "Float like a butterfly. Float like a butterfly. Float like a butterfly...." I gave her three because I did not think that one would be enough.

I also planted some daisies at the base of her diving board to help secure it to the pole, and I chose daisies because they are Lu Lu's favorite. You probably already knew that from her swimming cap and bathing suit.

Three-dimensional Effects

Just in case Lu Lu does actually make the jump into the tub of water that Skinny is holding for her, she's wearing 3-D flippers so she has no problems swimming.

Embellishments

All bathing suits should have a little something extra to help make us look pretty, so I gave Lu Lu's suit a ruffle around her neck.

Layout Options

If you want to create Lu Lu all by herself, she still needs a reason to wear that beautiful swimsuit. How about putting her up on a ladder and adding the tub from Skinny's pattern under her? She is just as likely to make that jump on her own as she is with Skinny holding the tub!

Three-dimensional Elements

Lu Lu's swimming flippers are constructed using the batting sandwich technique. Use the flipper patterns found on Lu Lu's pattern. I satin stitched them in place when stitching Lu Lu's foot. I further secured them by sewing a line down beside the satin-stitched seams while quilting. This prevented them from flopping around too much.

Cathy Wiggins

"Your heart will always be happy if you make others happy first."

Skinny

Laugh if you want to at Skinny's name. He doesn't mind because making people laugh is what makes his heart sing. Since Skinny is one of the larger clowns, I gave him the job of holding the water tub for Lu Lu. He said yes to the job because he knew that Lu Lu would never jump. It is not because Lu Lu is scared. You see, Skinny knows Lu Lu better than anybody else and he knows, for a fact, that Lu Lu would never get her new swimsuit wet.

Quilting Designs

In the event that she decides to dive, Lu Lu has insisted that Skinny fill the tank with salt water because she heard that it is easier to float in salt water. When filling the tank from the ocean, Skinny picked up some extra entertainment including a few fish and Maria, the mermaid.

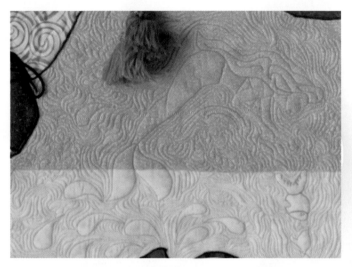

This extra entertainment, along with walking backwards, is causing Skinny to spill some water. I sure hope the water splashing on the path does not cause Bubbles problems on his unicycle!

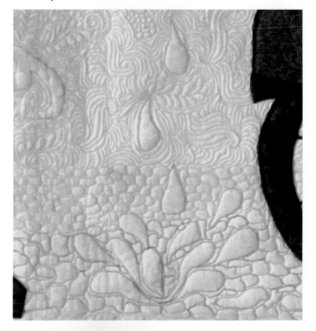

Three-dimensional Effects

It is tricky to walk backwards and carry the water tub, so Skinny wanted something simple for his 3-D effect. He was afraid that something big would catch too much wind, so I only gave him a 3-D hat band.

Embellishments

I gave Skinny a matching pom-pom ball on the tip of his hat, and what would an outfit of this size be without a pom-pom trim around the bottom?

Layout Options

If Skinny is your choice of clowns, and you really don't have a need for him to be holding a tub of water, have him juggling balls containing letters of the name of your favorite person or use Bubbles' bowling pins.

Three-dimensional Elements

I constructed the hatband using the batting sandwich technique. I added some decorative stitching on the top edge and attached it across Skinny's head and up the back.

"Everyone must learn to balance things in their life."

Little Bit

Little Bit is our busiest clown. It took us three tries to get all of those plates up on the poles once he was on the ball because his red nose kept falling off. I just don't understand how he can stay balanced on that ball with those big shoes on his feet!

Quilting Designs

Once the plates were in place, I had to put the teapot on the blue plate and the teacup on the green plate. Little Bit insisted that they go on those particular plates because that way the teacup could catch some of the water that the teapot is spraying. And how about all of those feathered wreaths that are falling off of the top plate? I just hope that he can hold on until the end of the parade!

Three-dimensional Effects

Have you ever seen suspenders and pants like Little Bit's before? He had them specially made for the parade. He has his jungle unitard on underneath just in case he loses his pants.

Embellishments

Wouldn't you know that once everything was in place, one of Little Bit's shoestrings came untied? So we had to double knot both of his shoestrings. And how do you like those big red buttons on his suspenders? He did have green ones, but they were not quite the right shade of green and Little Bit felt that they clashed with his hair.

Layout Options

I think that Little Bit would work well just as he is if you decide to give him his own quilt. You could use the patterns of the teapot, teacup, and wreath on page 31 and construct them out of fabric if you wish.

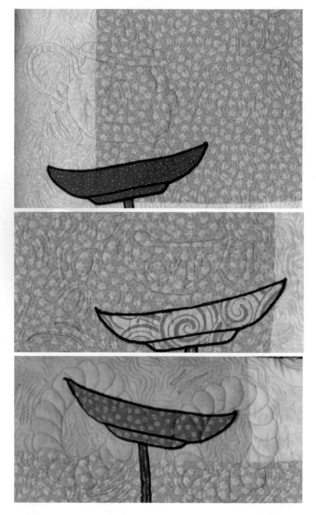

Three-dimensional Elements

The suspenders are made using the batting sandwich method. The suspenders are only attached at the top next to the collar. For his pants, I used a single piece of fabric and simply hemmed the top edge. They are attached on all sides except the top is left open.

"If you have great hair, show it to the world."

Bubbles

Bubbles is quite a talented clown. He loves to juggle with bowling pins that spell a happy message. That may not seem too exciting, but who else can do juggling while riding a unicycle? And if that is not enough, Bubbles is also pulling a wagon.

Quilting Designs

Bubbles did not want a large hat because it might get in his way when he is juggling. This does not mean that he can't have some decorations and adornments on top, so I added a few feathers and flowers. They are light and airy and should just blow in the wind while on the parade and not bother Bubbles' juggling in any way. I do hope that Bubbles is keeping an eye on the road because Skinny may be causing a problem with the water that he is spilling along the way.

If you look closely, you will see that Bubbles brought along his pet fishes. He placed them on the wagon right behind him and even put an umbrella over them so that they would not get too hot in the sun. I do hope that he is careful—some of the water is sloshing out!

Three-dimensional Effects

How about that wild red hair? It must have been quite a challenge to get that hat to stay on. It is great that Bubbles has matched his nose and lips to his hair perfectly.

Bubbles selected his outfit because he just loved the ruffle collar on the top. And because he pulls one of the parade wagons, he has a pull loop just like Hoss.

Embellishments

Bubbles is so decorated that he did not require any additional embellishments. He did, however, need to have a rope to attach to the wagon.

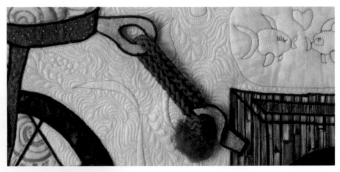

Layout Options

If your Bubbles will not be pulling a wagon, he will not need the pull loop. He can be juggling anything from bowling pins to ducks. I have included all of the letters in the alphabet on page 76–77 so you can spell out any name or message that you would like to include on the pins.

Three-dimensional Elements

Bubble's hair is constructed using several triangle-shaped batting sandwiches. They are attached with satin stitching around his face.

His ruffle collar is made from a U-shaped pattern that is a bit longer than the distance around his neck, using fabric only, and folded during the satin stitching to form the ruffles. You can use the collar found on the pattern on page 34 as your guide.

34

"You are never too old to swing."

Boo Boo
Believe me, there was quite a bit of discussion as to who was going to swing on the swing during the parade! Boo Boo won out because he is the clumsiest of all the clowns and it was felt that everyone, including those watching the parade, would be safer if he was to ride in the swing!

Quilting Designs

When Boo Boo was asked what he would like to have hanging down beside him from the pole, he thought for a moment and then asked for a string of roses because they are his favorite flower. He knew that the ladies would love the soft fragrance of them as the parade passed by.

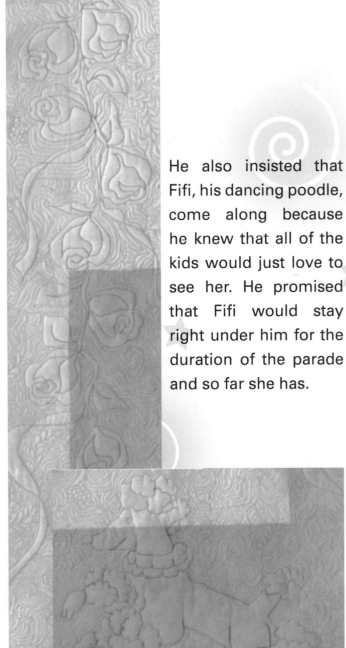

He also insisted that Fifi, his dancing poodle, come along because he knew that all of the kids would just love to see her. He promised that Fifi would stay right under him for the duration of the parade and so far she has.

Three-dimensional Effects

We decided to add a ruffle collar to Boo Boo's shirt to bring out the colors in the sleeves. With sleeves that big, he really did need a big collar!

Embellishments

Of course, a simple white rope would not do for his swing. Boo Boo wanted a rope that would match his costume and very large, over-sized buttons were a must. Because of the expense of the colorful rope, white rope was used to make the loops around the pole from which the swing hangs.

Layout Options

Boo Boo would look perfect on a quilt of his own hanging from loops placed on the top border of your quilt.

Three-dimensional Elements

Boo Boo's ruffle collar is made from a U-shaped pattern that is a bit longer than the distance around his neck, using fabric only, and folded during the satin stitching to form the ruffles. You can use the collar found on page 38 as your guide.

38 Cathy Wiggins

"Don't ever take the easy way out. It's just not as fun."

Yum Yum   Boy, was there a big question over whether or not Yum Yum could actually stand on his hands for the entire parade! He was determined that he could, but to help him out, it was suggested that maybe he should use a few helium balloons tied to his ankles. So that is what he did and, so far, he has maintained his handstand.

Quilting Designs

Pablo's little friend, Roberto Rat, wanted to join the parade because he could balance on a ball. The only place he could find to perform was on the pole beside Yum Yum. This made Yum Yum happy because you don't get to see a rat in a tutu balancing on top of a ball every day!

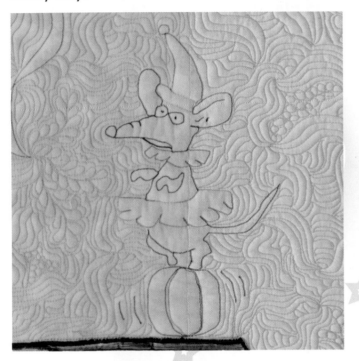

Three-dimensional Effects

Yum Yum was not about to make the trip without his lucky green hat. He has worn it in every parade so far.

Embellishments

Yum Yum replaced the green pom-pom at the tip of his hat before the parade started. And he personally selected the colors for the ribbons that tie the balloons to his ankles.

Layout Options

When considering placing Yum Yum on his own quilt, how about using the alphabet found on pages 76–77 to add a name or message on the balloons? You can use the pattern of Roberto Rat on page 43 and make him out of fabric. You could also use one of Lu Lu's butterflies on page 23. Just remember when designing your quilt layout, Yum Yum does need something to look at during the trip.

Three-dimensional Elements

Yum Yum's hat is made using the batting sandwich method. Use the band from the pattern as a template and a triangle shape for the top of the hat. The hat from the pattern can be used as a guide.

Yum Yum

Cathy Wiggins   43   Clowns on Parade

"Sunshine and music help make the world go around."

Sunshine
Everyone knew that Sunshine would be joining the parade to provide the music. We just had to figure out where in the world she was going to ride. It would be way too boring for her to just walk along behind the rest of the clowns, so why not hang her right in the middle of the action?

(Sunshine does have a little concern that if and when Lu Lu decides to jump, she might get taken out along the way, so they worked out a signal between themselves so Lu Lu can let Sunshine know when she is coming through.)

Quilting Designs

You will always know when Sunshine is playing music because you can see the musical notes and air flowing out of her horn. She uses this magic horn so even those folks watching the parade who have trouble hearing will know that she is playing music.

Three-dimensional Effects

Sunshine always dyes her hair some bright color from the rainbow before each parade, and she has chosen blue for this one. She wanted it to look, from Lu Lu's viewpoint, like waves of water so it would blend in with the water from Skinny's tank. Why? I don't know!

Embellishments

Sunshine, like Little Bit, double-knotted her shoe laces before she was suspended from the pole so she would not have to worry about her shoes coming off. (She borrowed the shoes, and they are a little too big.) She selected the orange rope because she loved the tassels.

Layout Options

Just as with Yum Yum, Sunshine can be hanging from the top border of her own quilt, and you could have letters for a message coming out of her horn instead of musical notes, either quilted or constructed from fabric.

Three-dimensional Elements

Sunshine's hair is made using the satin-stitch fusible technique. I cut several wave shapes and layered them as I satin stitched her face.

Clowns on Parade

Pablo How could we have a parade of clowns without a monkey somewhere!? Pablo wanted to bring all of his friends from the barrel (of monkeys), but decided to bring his maracas instead so that he could play along with Sunshine.

Quilting Designs

I think that Pablo is the smartest one in the parade because he knew that this parade would be traveling a long way and he brought along a bunch of bananas for snacks. He also knew how much Lu Lu loves flowers, so he hung a basket of nice flowers from the end of his pole for Lu Lu to enjoy.

Embellishments

Pablo was hoping for a Spanish fiesta-themed parade, so he came wearing his signature sombrero with the red pom-poms.

Layout Options

How about making three Pablos? Move their arms and tails around, and have a whole band of monkeys playing maracas.

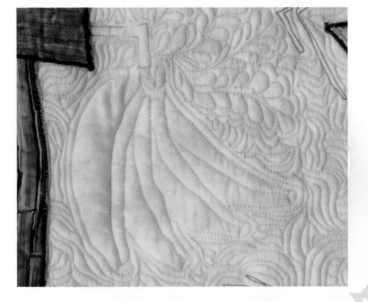

I used stencil SCL-290-08 from the Stencil Company for the flowers Pablo hung for LuLu.

Letters, Wagons, Sign, and Poles

Besides the clowns and Pablo, there were all sorts of additional elements designed for the parade. You may choose to include any or all of them in your quilt.

There is a two-wheeled wagon and a four-wheeled wagon, each carrying a pole for the clowns to ride on. I constructed my wagons and poles using woodgrain fabric and then used the printed woodgrain as my guide for quilting. I used the same size wheels on both wagons and simply satin stitched the wheel spokes. I used the same pulls as those found on Hoss and Bubbles.

Notice how I used a different fabric for the inside of each wagon, both of which are visible. This helps to give the illusion that you can see inside the wagons.

The poles are all constructed using the same woodgrain fabric, and I topped each with a small platform. Again, I used the woodgrain of the fabric as my guide for quilting.

To give the illusion that the horizontal poles are going into the vertical poles, I curved the ends slightly, defining the curve with satin stitching.

I used woodgrain fabric for the poles.

I used a skinnier vertical pole from which to hang the sign. You could use a small quilt top for the sign, if you wish.

I used preprinted quilted fabric for the sign.

I have added feathers and swirls coming from the top of the wagon. And remember, Bubbles placed his fish tank on top of the two-wheeled wagon.

The letters used on the sign are the same size and style as those found on the bowling pins that Bubbles is juggling. These same letters can be used anywhere in your quilt top design.

I have not included patterns for the poles. You can just cut them the length that you need and add the top platform.

Use either or both of the wagons for your quilt. Once the wagons are in place, satin stitch the spokes of the wheels.

Use the pull pattern to make your own three-dimensional pulls using the satin-stitch fusible technique.

The letters on pages 76–77 can be used for any purpose on your quilt. I used them on the bowling pins that Bubbles is juggling, on the sign, and I also used them when I quilted the names of the clowns. I wanted them to appear as if they had been handwritten with a crayon.

Ruffle Border

Because of the size limitations of the quilt, I had to be creative with a border. I decided to use the same ruffle design that I used for some of the clowns' costume collars and I repeated all of the clown costume fabric. I wanted the ruffle design to be random and fun. Here is how I made it:

1. Determine the length of the border needed by measuring the edge of the quilt. Double this number.

2. Cut pieces 7" wide ranging from 6" to 12" in length.

3. Sew these pieces together until the desired border length (from step 1) is reached.

4. Fold the border strip wrong sides together and press.

5. Beginning at one corner, sew the raw edge of the strip to the top edge of the quilt, periodically folding the strip on top of itself to form a ruffle. I sewed my ruffles randomly with some folds on top and some underneath, varying the folds each time. I found it much easier to make the ruffles random than to try and make them all the same size.

6. I sewed the two sides first and then the top and bottom, overlapping the side ruffles in the corners.

This is the border that I chose to put on my quilt. Let your imagination help you plan your fun border. Just remember to think out of the box sometimes.

Batting and Quilting

Batting

As for most of my show quilts, I used two layers of batting. I have found that this works best both for the handling and hanging of the quilt and for showing off all of the quilting designs in the background.

❋ My base layer (the layer next to the quilt backing) is Quilters Dream White Poly Request. The Quilters Dream Poly is a great choice for wallhangings because it holds together where, sometimes, cotton may tend to stretch and separate.

❋ My top layer (the layer next to the quilt top) is Hobbs Heirloom® wool. The Hobbs wool is fantastic for showing off the quilting designs. It is a somewhat dense batt that maintains its density, fills the quilting designs, and holds its shape through the handling received on the show circuit.

Neither of these batts holds folds from shipping and stacking like cotton batts or other wools tend to do. By using these two batts, you can achieve a faux trapunto look without the cutting and stuffing.

Thread

There are many factors involved when deciding which threads to use for quilting.

For this quilt, I had one goal in mind: I wanted all of my quilting designs to stand out and be seen by the viewer. To achieve this I knew that I had to

1. use a thicker thread for the designs themselves; and

2. use dense quilting in the background to make the designs "poof" up.

I use Superior Threads for quilting almost exclusively. On this quilt I used their 40-weight Rainbows™ thread for the designs and their 50-weight Bottom Line™ thread for the background quilting and in the bobbin. I always match my bobbin thread with my top thread. So every time I change threads on the top, I put in a new bobbin color as well. This helps eliminate the "pokies" on top and on the back of the quilt.

Quilting Designs

I quilted CLOWNS ON PARADE in three passes on my longarm machine. On the first pass, I quilted around all of the elements on the quilt top including the clowns, poles, and wagons. This stabilized the quilt so that I could take it off of the machine to quilt other quilts if I needed to. This pass also secured my backing, so I would not have to worry about creating any pleats.

On pass two, I quilted in all of the designs found in the spaces around the clowns.

I added ribbons and feathers coming out of the top of the pole. This further stabilized the quilt.

On the third pass, I quilted in all of the background using the 50-weight Bottom Line thread. I used this thread so that the quilting stitches would disappear into the quilt, leaving only the texture visible from the light and shadows.

As you can see from this close-up photograph, I selected a modified McTavish design. In between the curves and echoes, I added pebbles and feathers randomly.

I used a pebble design to create a texture for the road that the parade is marching on. I started with larger pebbles next to the bottom border on the foreground and made them smaller as I went further up the quilt.

I also used a dark variegated thread to give the illusion of shadows on the road.

Binding and Blocking

There are many books on the market and quite a few web sites that can give you step-by-step instructions on both binding and blocking a quilt. I have included some tips and ideas on the problems that I had constructing this quilt and what I did to resolve them.

Binding

I had some problems with the binding on this quilt. That was one area where I always got "needs improvement" comments on every show critique sheet. I finally realized that I had cut my binding fabric too small. I usually cut my bindings 2½ inches wide for a double binding. However, in order to be able to easily fold the binding over the ruffled border, I had to cut it 3 inches wide. So, after about a year of showing CLOWNS ON PARADE, I completely replaced the binding, and I never had another negative comment.

Blocking

Because of the fusible web I used on CLOWNS ON PARADE in addition to the heavy quilting, there was no way that this quilt was going to lie flat. I had to block it, and this was going to be a problem because it was too big to put in my washing machine, plus, I did not have a space large enough to lay it out.

For most of my quilts, once the quilting is done and my binding is on, I put the quilt in my washing machine on the rinse cycle of the delicate setting in cold water. But since this quilt would not fit, I laid it out on the floor in my brother's house (he has the space that I don't have) on top of a clean sheet and sprayed it with water until it was damp all over.

Then, starting in one corner using T-pins and a large square ruler, I pinned the quilt corner down to the carpet and padding. Working out towards one of the adjoining corners, I straightened the edge of the quilt, pinning as I went. I then squared that corner and kept going until I had the whole quilt square and all sides straight.

Once the edges of the quilt were straight and pinned, I had all sorts of problems in the center of the quilt where things were not lying flat. To solve these issues, I pinned them all down. I used hundreds of pins, and when I was finished, the whole quilt was pinned flat on the floor. I then laid a clean sheet on top of the quilt and let it dry. It dried within a few hours.

If you don't have a brother with lots of empty floor space, you can use insulation boards from a home improvement store. They are 8 feet by 4 feet, so get as many as you need to fit your quilt and tape them together using duct tape. Place them outside on a sunny day and repeat my steps above. If you lay your quilt out in the morning, it should be dry by nightfall.

It is important to block any quilt before it goes to a show. Squaring and blocking is the only way to ensure that it will hang straight.

These projects will show you just how flexible these clown patterns are and how you can easily apply them to many of your own creations.

Each project uses a different size pattern. The enlargement size needed is given at the beginning of each project. Any office supply store can produce these enlargements for you.

It is difficult to determine the exact amount of fabric needed to construct the clowns for these projects because it depends on the size of the enlargement of the clown pattern and how the fabrics will be used within the patterns. I used up all of my brightly colored scraps for my clowns.

For each project I have listed the different sections of the pattern requiring fabrics. You can choose to repeat fabrics or use entirely different fabrics for each section of the clowns.

Clown patterns can be enlarged to fit into many different creative projects.

Tote size: 17½" x 17½" x 5" with two outside pockets and three inside pockets.

Since Lu Lu loves being seen in her swim suit, what better way to let her show off than to put her on her own vacation tote!? And since she does not mind sharing the spotlight, I decided to put the mermaid from the background quilting patterns of Skinny, along with her fish, on the other side.

This fashionable tote has three inside pockets: a 5" x 5" and an 8" x 8" on one side, and a roomy 10" x 10" on the other side. It also has two outside pockets measuring 9" x 12" each.

Pattern Size

Lu Lu is 100% the size of the pattern found in the book. No enlarging is needed.

Enlarge the mermaid and the fish patterns 125%.

Fabric Requirements

Clown Fabrics

Brightly colored fabric pieces for sections of Lu Lu, the mermaid, and the fish

For Lu Lu you need scrap fabrics for:
Swimsuit
2 different fabrics for her flippers
Skin • Nose • Lips
Swim cap
White and black for her eyes and around the mouth
Piece of muslin slightly larger than the pattern
For the mermaid and fish you need scrap fabrics for:
Tail • Fins • Swimsuit top
Hair • Skin • Eye
2 different fabrics for the fish
Pieces of muslin slightly larger than the patterns

Tote Outside Fabric

I chose to use heavyweight outdoor fabric for my tote.

Front and back panels – 18" x 18", cut 2
Side and bottom panels – 18" x 5½", cut 3
Outside pockets – 10" x 12½", cut 4

Tote Lining Fabric

Front and back panels – 18″ x 18″, cut 2
Side panels – 18″ x 5½", cut 3
Inside pockets – 5½" x 5½", cut 2
8½" x 8½", cut 2
10½" x 10½", cut 2

Handles

2 lengths of handle or satchel webbing cut 40" long or to your desired length.

Step-by-Step

1. Construct Lu Lu, the mermaid, and the fish according to the Let's Get Started chapter on pages 6–11, and trim the muslin from each.

2. With rights sides together, sew 5½" inside pocket squares together, using a ¼" seam.

Leave the fourth side open for turning.

4. Turn right-side out, fold the edges inside ½" and press.

Top stitch the remaining opening used for turning with a ¼" seam.

5. Repeat this process with the 8½" and 10½" inside pocket squares. The inside pockets are now complete.

6. Center Lu Lu onto one of the 10" x 12½" outside pocket panels.

Lu Lu is sewn into the center of the outside pocket panel with a satin stitch.

7. With right sides together, sew the Lu Lu pocket panel and another panel together on three sides, using a ¼" seam. Leave the top side open for turning.

8. Turn the panel right-side out, fold the edges inside ½", press and top stitch using a ¼" seam.

9. Pin the pocket panel onto the right side of the outside front panel according to the diagram and sew it on all sides using a ¼"seam.

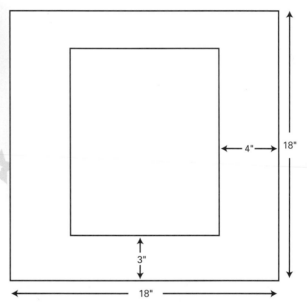

Sew the outside pockets, leaving the tops of the pockets open.

10. Place the mermaid and fish into position. Satin stitch them into place. Repeat steps 7, 8, and 9 above, except use the outside back panel.

11. Pin the inside pocket panels onto the right sides of the lining using a ¼" seam.

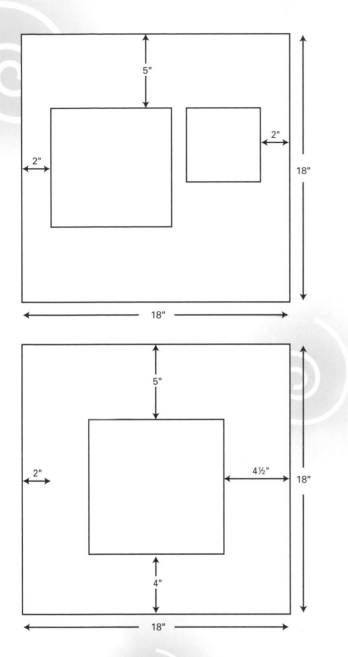

Position the inside pockets and sew, leaving the tops of the pockets open.

12. Place the Lu Lu outside panel and the lining panel with the single pocket right sides together, making sure the open ends of the pockets are all facing in the same direction. Sew together using a ¼" seam, leaving the bottom open for turning.

13. Turn the panel right-side out, fold the edges inside ½", press and top stitch using a ¼" seam.

The Lu Lu panel is complete.

14. Repeat steps 12 and 13 with the mermaid and fish outside panel and the other lining panel.

15. Place the outside side panel and lining side panel together. Sew them, using a ¼" seam, leaving one short side open for turning.

16. Turn the panels right-side out, fold the edges inside ½", press and top stitch them using a ¼" seam.

17. Repeat steps 11 and 12 with the other side panel and the bottom panel. Now your tote pieces are completed.

Now you are ready to build your tote.

18. Place the Lu Lu panel and side panel outsides together and sew. Repeat with the other side and bottom panels.

Sew the side panels and the bottom panel to the Lu Lu panel.

19. With outsides together and the pocket opening at the top, sew the mermaid panel to one side panel using a ¼" seam. Repeat with other side panel and bottom. Now your tote should be inside out with the short seams between the bottom and side open. Pin these together and sew using a ¼" seam.

Now sew the sides and bottom together.

20. Attach strap webbing onto the Lu Lu side of the tote sewing ¼" from the edge of the webbing in a rectangle shape to secure. You may wish to sew crisscross as well. Repeat with a second strap onto the mermaid side of the tote.

Stitch the strap webbing securely to both panels of your tote.

Note: Use a stiff interfacing between the outside panels and the lining panels if you would like a stiffer tote.

Yum Yum seemed to be the perfect clown for a floor pillow. With his hands and legs outstretched he can either be standing tall on his feet or playing around doing handstands.

Pattern Size

The size of the finished pillow depends on the enlargement size of the pattern. For a pillow that is 30" before it is stuffed, use a 350% enlargement. I decided to try one larger and had my pattern enlarged 700%; the finished pillow is 40" long.

Completed pillows are 30" (pink) and 40" (yellow/green), respectively.

Fabric Requirements

Unlike the other projects, this pillow will require large scraps. Depending on just how big you go, you may need as much as a fat quarter size, since you will want to use the same fabrics on the front of Yum Yum as on the back. Assorted bright colored fabrics are needed as follows:

Yum Yum front and back

    Pants

    3 fabrics for his shoes

        (shoe top, sides of soles, soles)

    3 fabrics for his shirt

        (body, sleeves, cuffs)

    Belt • Collar

    3 fabrics for his hat

        (brim, body, ball)

    Skin • Hair • Nose, lips • Cheeks

Two muslin rectangles large enough to cover the patterns

Other Supplies

Stuffing of your choice adequate to fill the completed pillow

Embellishments such as buttons, fuzzyballs, shoe strings, etc.

Step-by-Step

1. Construct the front and back of Yum Yum according to the Let's Get Started chapter on pages 6–11 with one exception: when tracing the pattern onto the reverse sides (Step 2), add ¼" to the outside edges. This will allow for the seam allowance needed when sewing the front and the back of the pillow together.

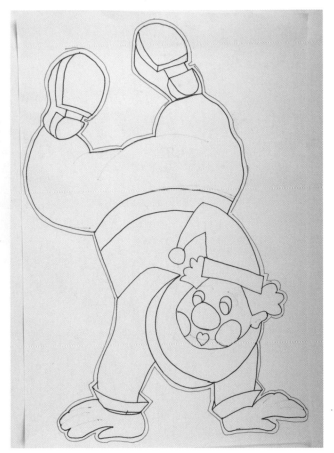

Add ¼" for the seam allowance all around the outside of both the front and back patterns.

2. Pin the front and back of a completed Yum Yum wrong sides together. Trim the muslin and some of the fabric edges as needed to ensure that the edges of both pieces match.)

Trimming with the wrong sides pinned together will give you an even edge to sew.

3. Re-pin the front and back of completed Yum Yum right sides together and sew with a ¼" to ½" seam. Leave an opening between his legs for turning.

4. Turn and stuff Yum Yum, making sure to fill all of the nooks and crannies with stuffing.

Using a wooden spoon handle works great for getting into the shoes and hands.

5. Once stuffing is complete, handsew the opening closed.

Note: Add embellishments either before stuffing or after, depending on if it will be sewn on or glued. For example, the buttons are sewn on before the sides are sewn together and the fuzzy balls are glued on after the stuffing is complete.

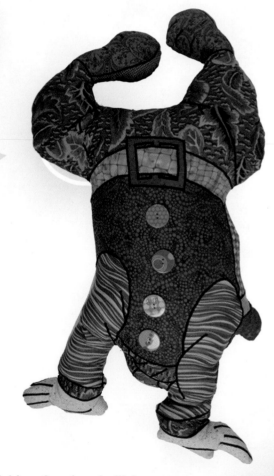

Add optional embellishments to your pillow such as real buttons on the shirt, a fuzzy ball on the hat ,or real shoestrings on the shoes.

Finished size: 27″ x 64″

Lu Lu and Skinny seem to be the perfect pair of clowns for a growth chart design. This project is simple and easy using a store-bought measuring tape for use on the pole and satin stitch appliqué. I chose to have my pole measure from 18" in height to 5'. You can make yours any height you wish. You can also change the wording on your growth chart to include a child's name.

Pattern Size

Lu Lu and Skinny are enlarged 150% from the pattern in the book.

The balloons and Lu Lu's diving board patterns are at 100%.

The water bucket is enlarged 150%.

The water drops are 100%.

The letters are enlarged 400%.

Fabric Requirements

Background fabric

a pieced or solid background measuring 27" x 64"

Pole

Brown fabric

Pole – 2 ½"" x 43" strip

Base – 2½" x 5" rectangle

Top – 2" x 4" rectangle

Light brown fabric for the writing strip – 1 ¼" x 43"

Clowns

For Lu Lu you need scrap fabrics for:

Swimsuit

2 fabrics for the flippers

Swim cap

Skin • Nose • Lips

White and black for the eyes and around the mouth

Pieces of muslin slightly larger than the patterns

For Skinny, you need scrap fabric for:

3 fabrics for his shirt

2 fabrics for his hat

3 fabrics for his shoes

Pants

Black and white for his eyes and mouth

Skin • Cheek • Nose

Skinny's water tub

Blue for the water and water drops

Brown for the tub

Gold for the bands

Piece of muslin slightly larger than the pattern

Scraps for red, blue, green and purple for the diving board, balloons, and letters

Binding

either a pieced binding measuring 190" or ⅓ yard cut to 2½" wide

Backing

32" x 68"

Sleeve

27" x 8½" folded in half to make a 4" sleeve.

Other Supplies

Measuring tape at least 5 feet long

Permanent fabric glue

Step-by-Step

1. Construct Skinny, his water tub, and Lu Lu according to the Let's Get Started chapter on pages 6–11, and individual patterns.

2. Trim the muslin from each completed pattern.

3. Create the letters, balloons, water drops, and diving board. DO NOT iron these pieces onto muslin.

4. Cut fusible web to fit the reverse side of each section of the pole and apply it to the back side of the pole fabric pieces.

5. Place your background fabric on a pressing surface and press the pole, its top and base, the diving board, balloons, letters, and water drops into place according to the diagram following the fusible web manufacturer's directions. Here is the complete layout of the quilt top. Your layout may vary depending on the wording you use.

6. Cut the measuring tape just short of the 18" and just past the 5' mark. Using the permanent fabric glue, attach the tape to the pole, using the diagram for placement.

7. Satin stitch around all objects except the measuring tape.

8. Using the photo for reference, pin Lu Lu in place and satin stitch her to

the background. Repeat with Skinny and his water tub.

Your top is now complete and ready for quilting. You may choose to add the flowers and butterflies Lu Lu had in the original CLOWNS ON PARADE quilt when you are quilting.

Feel free to add embellishments to your growth chart, once it is complete. I have added ribbons on my balloons and a fuzz ball on Skinny's hat.

Hanging Directions

Do not forget to add a sleeve for hanging! I sew the top of my sleeve to the back as I attach my binding. Then I hand stitch it down as I hand stitch my binding.

For extra touches, you can add fuzzy balls to the clowns' noses and to the top of Skinny's hat. You can also tie a marking pin to a string and attach it the back of Lu Lu's diving board. Use the light brown fabric on the pole to mark the growth of your child.

For accurate measurement of your child, hang your chart so that the bottom of the measuring tape is 18" from the floor.

Aa Bb Cc

Dd Ee Ff

Gg Hh Ii Jj

Kk Ll Mm

Cathy Wiggins was born and raised in eastern North Carolina were she received degrees in mathematics and software engineering. She spent 20 years in the telecommunications industry in product development and marketing, traveling the world to help bring cellular and wireless communications into everyday life.

Even though her education is in technology, her love has always been art and any form of creativity. During her years in telecommunications she continued to foster her love of art through taking numerous workshops on subjects such as sculpting, pottery, and all forms of painting. She eventually settled on using acrylic paints on paper as her medium of choice.

Through experimenting and practice, Cathy developed her own style of painting where she would, through the use of value and layers of paint, interpret photographs on paper. She won numerous awards locally

and nationally for her work and began teaching her technique to others.

In October of 2002 she left the high-tech world. She and her family moved to Lake Gaston, North Carolina, where Cathy was introduced to quilting by a neighbor. In February of 2003, she attended her first national quilt show and knew then that she had found a home. This is when she really discovered just how vast and creative the world of quilting really is. She came home and immediately began work on a quilt, applying the same ideas of using values to interpret photographs in quilt design.

The following year that quilt was juried into the AQS Paducah show and Cathy knew this was what she was supposed to be doing with her life. Since that time she has won many national and international awards for her quilts and is teaching her design techniques as well as holding inspirational workshops to help others realize their goals and dreams.

Now Cathy has taken her quilting work a step further with her "Just for Fun" series of quilts. She still uses the same design techniques she uses when she is working with photographs, but now she creates quilts that are both whimsical and humorous.

When asked why she has made this shift in her work, Cathy says, "I just want to create quilts for the pure fun of it. I want to create quilts that bring smiles to the faces of the viewers and designs that are ageless, things that remind us of our childhood." In addition to writing articles for magazines and traveling nationally to teach, with the success of her Just for Fun series of quilts, she is now writing books and creating patterns based on her award-winning quilts.

Cathy lives with her husband, Randy, daughter, Olivia, their dogs, Stella and Walter, and their parrot, Alex.

The End